Famous Birds of the Bible
Six Studies for Personal Devotion or Small Groups

Brant D. Baker

Cover: Original watercolor by Kathi Rippe
All Scripture quotes from the NRSV unless otherwise noted

Table of Contents

Famous Birds of the Ark

DISCUSS/REFLECT

What is your favorite bird and why?

READ

Genesis 8:6-12

DISCUSS/REFLECT

What questions does this passage raise for you?

READ

Most of us know at least a little about doves, or at least doves in the Bible. They appear prominently in the life of Jesus, associated with his birth, his baptism, and in his ministry. Around the time of his birth we are told that Mary and Joseph sacrificed two doves at the Temple as proscribed by the law (Luke 2:24). At his baptism we are told (in all four gospels) that after Jesus came up out of the water, the Holy Spirit came and descended on him "like a dove" (Matthew 3:16, Mark 1:10, Luke 3:22, John 1:32). In his ministry Jesus overturns the tables of those selling doves in the temple (Matthew 21:12–17, Mark 11:15–19, Luke 19:45–48 [doves are not specified], and John 2:16).

Lessor known facts about doves include that the cooooOOOOO-woo-woo-woo call is almost always made by the male bird, and is a mating call. Pairs tend to mate for life, and when it comes time, the female almost always lays just two eggs. From there both mom and dad work to feed their new babies something called "pigeon milk," which is secreted by the parents in their crop lining, but by the fourth day the kids are starting to eat seeds. (birdsandblooms.com/blog/10-surprising-facts-about-mourning-doves/).

A group of doves is a "dule," a "dole," or a "piteousness." Compare these innocuous terms to those used for misunderstood and maligned ravens, which in a group is called an "unkindness" or sometimes a "conspiracy." Writing in his classic *Smith's Bible Dictionary* (1901), Dr. William Smith said, "There is something weird and shrewd in the expression of the raven's countenance, a union of cunning and malignity which may have contributed to give it among widely-revered nations a reputation for preternatural knowledge." Some cultures have believed ravens were the souls of wicked priests (and crows the souls of wicked nuns!). In some places a raven that croaked at night was thought to be the soul of a murder victim, or an exorcized spirits. Perhaps because ravens feed on carrion, some have even imagined that ravens flying overhead were themselves a harbinger of death (mentalfloss.com/article/53295/ 10-fascinating-facts-about-ravens).

The truth is that ravens are pretty remarkable. They are extremely maneuverable in the air, along the lines of falcons and hawks. Besides carrion, they can survive on a wide range of foods, from berries to nuts, from mice to insects, from eggs to worms. They have been known to hunt in teams, and to call other predators when unable to open a carcass on their own. Ravens are believed to mate for life and build nests according to their terrain (stick nests in forests, rock nests in deserts), with both parents caring for their young. They typically make a croaking sound, but have a wide range of expressive sounds and calls Ravens are also thought to be among the most intelligent birds, and have shown the ability to learn complex tasks and employ logic in solving problems, in some tests doing better even than chimpanzees. This high intelligence also makes ravens rather playful and even a bit mischievous (nationalgeographic.com/common-raven, and news.softpedia. com/10-Amazing-Facts-About-Ravens).

In Scripture we find ravens most prominently in the flood account in Genesis, and in the story of Elijah found in 1 Kings 17 (see next study). In Job 38:41 and Psalm 147:9 they are mentioned as one for whom God provides. These are the passages Jesus might have had in mind when he said, "Consider the ravens: they neither sow nor reap, they have neither storehouse nor barn, and yet God feeds them. Of how much more value are you than the birds! (Luke 12:24). More severely, we read in Proverbs 30:17, "The eye that mocks a father and scorns to obey a mother will be pecked out by the ravens of the valley and eaten by the vultures" (this, by the way, is an attack habit of eagles, vultures, and hawks as well).

DISCUSS/REFLECT

What is your personal opinion of both doves and ravens, and is that opinion based on first-hand experience or something else? Which do you like the most?

READ

In dealing with this story in Genesis the first and most obvious question is, "why two birds?" The dominant historical interpretation assigns the raven to the "fallen" earth (as it feeds on carrion), and the dove the "new" earth God seeks to establish. But this unclean/clean, vice/virtue, failure/success, wild/gentle rendering, while intriguing, doesn't really seem to explain why Noah sent out two different species at two different times.

More contemporary commentators suggest that two sources have here been combined into one story (unlike, for example, in Genesis 1 and 2, where two sources have apparently been kept separate, and each given its own place). This line of interpretation suggests that whoever combined the two accounts, one that featured a raven, one that featured a dove, was reluctant to remove either. What is important, these commentators suggest, is not the bird but the activity of Noah sending out some kind of bird to investigate the land. As a result, there is no symbolism or meaning to be read into the different birds.

The issue grows slightly more complex when the three-fold movement of this part of the story is noted. There are two different birds, but three trips. So, what is important, the three trips or the two birds? It is a math question of epic proportion!

An interesting suggestion comes from R.W.L. Moberly, professor of theology and biblical interpretation at Durham University, who notes the movement of the raven seems to be continuous and ongoing in the original Hebrew. He notes further that the continuous movement of the raven in Genesis 8:7 ("it went to and fro until the waters were dried up from the earth") is very similar to the movement of the wind in Genesis 8:1 ("And God made a wind blow over the earth, and the waters subsided..."), which in turn seems to find parallel to the movement of the wind in

Genesis 1:2 ("the earth was a formless void and darkness covered the face of the deep, while a wind from God swept over the face of the waters."). Both Genesis 1:2 and Genesis 8:1 indicate that the *ruah* (spirit, wind) of God is present at moments of creation and new creation (see also Deuteronomy 32:11-12, where the same verb is used to describe the movement of an eagle that "hovers" over its young: "As an eagle stirs up its nest, and hovers over its young; as it spreads its wings, takes them up, and bears them aloft on its pinions, the Lord alone guided him; no foreign god was with him."). "Thus we are to imagine a barren watery waste over which God's spirit moves to and fro like a bird," says Dr. Moberly, "representing the divine power which will transform the waste into a habitable world. Noah's act of sending out the raven, therefore, is a kind of imitation of God" (353).

Of course, the association with the Spirit of God as a raven, rather than as a dove (as at Jesus' baptism), is perhaps a bit troubling, given all of the negative associations people have with ravens, and Moberly admits he doesn't quite understand why it would be this bird, rather than the later dove, that would be given this role.

Regardless, the take away from the story seems to be that just as God was present at creation, so God is present in the new creation, and Noah's action in sending the raven could be understood as an act of worship, a remembrance or reenactment of God's creative Spirit at work in bringing order out of chaos, peace out of destruction. Even as he is going about the practical matter of determining the state of the land (with the dove), Noah keeps before him a reminder of the presence of God (with the raven) ("Why Did Noah Send out a Raven?" *Vetus Testamentum,* Vol. 50, Fasc. 3, July 2000, pp. 345-356).

DISCUSS/REFLECT

Do you find it easy or difficult to associate the raven in Genesis 8 with the spirit of God hovering over the waters of chaos before creation/new creation? What alternative ideas do you have as to why there might be two birds in this account?

READ

Sailors of old used doves and other birds to help them find and navigate toward land. But Noah was neither a sailor, a boat builder, or a zoo keeper when he was asked by God to build the ark. So why did God choose Noah to build that ark? It was due to his righteousness, which inclined him to *obedience*. The Bible tells us that, *"Noah did all that God commanded him."* This refrain is repeated twice, once in Genesis 6:22, and again in Genesis 7:5. Being useful in service to God doesn't mean we know everything we need to know, or that we get it all right, it simply means that we are willing to *try* to get it all right in obedience to God's call. Instead of saying, "I don't know what I'm doing," or "I've already done my share," we are invited to say, *"Here I am, send me"* (Isaiah 6:8).

A second lesson from Noah has to do with *faithfulness,* staying obedient over the long haul. In the great eleventh chapter of Hebrews that lists many of the faithful servants of God over the ages, we are told *"By faith Noah...built an ark...and became an heir to the righteousness that is in accordance with faith."* (11:7). How long did Noah remain faithful? Someone has calculated that it took Noah 120 years to build this floating zoo, and we can imagine that in that time he endured a fair amount of self-doubt, a fair amount of fatigue, and a fair amount ridicule from those around him. Presbyterian pastor, writer, and scholar Eugene Peterson has called this kind of faithfulness *"a long obedience in the same direction."*

Noah also shows that we should stay fit, because when we're over 500 years old (or maybe just 88), God might ask us to do something big. Why might God sometimes have a preference for someone a bit older? Perhaps because they are less likely to worry about critics, and more likely to just get on with the job that needs to be done.

And of course, no matter what storms we might endure in life and in service to God, there's always a rainbow waiting. God is faithful, and at the conclusion of Noah's story we are told that his first act upon touching dry ground was to build an altar to the Lord. *"Noah built an altar to the Lord... and offered burnt offerings..."* (Genesis 8:20). Noah sacrificed some of the animals, and in response to this act of thanksgiving God promises to never again destroy the earth and gives the promise of the rainbow.

DISCUSS/REFLECT

Which of the lessons from Noah's example are most meaningful to you in this season of your life? Why? What might be God calling you to do, and how can you take inspiration from Noah's story?

PRAYER

Conclude your time in prayer with and for one another.

Consider the Ravens

DISCUSS/REFLECT

So, seriously, how are you feeling about ravens by now?

READ

1 Kings 17:1-7

DISCUSS/REFLECT

What questions does this passage raise for you?

READ

Our first introduction to Elijah in Scripture comes as he is telling King Ahab the news that God is sending a drought to the land. Upon giving this message it seems wise for Elijah to get out of town, so God sends him to hide by Kerith Brook, close to where it joined the Jordan River. Scholars debate the location of this brook, as they also debate the location of Tishbe (where Elijah was from), because that's what scholars do.

The initial arrangement is that the ravens will bring Elijah food. Bread and meat arrive each morning and evening (apparently Elijah had a ravenous appetite!), and he drinks from the brook until it dries up on account of the aforementioned drought.

It's worth noting that being fed by a raven would be difficult for a good Jew like Elijah. According to Leviticus 11:15, ravens are unclean (along with eagles, vultures, various owls, and hawks). It may be that ravens are unclean, along with these others, because they consume carrion. Be that as it may, God sends this particular bird to feed His prophet. "God chose what is low and despised in the world, things that are not, to reduce to nothing things that are, so that no one might boast in the presence of God" (1 Corinthians 1:28-29).

Elijah may know that his next meal will be provided by the ravens, but it is probably safe to say that ravens generally don't know where their next meal is coming from. In fact, this is pretty much what Jesus *does* say in Luke 12:24, "Consider the ravens: they neither sow nor reap, they have neither storehouse nor barn, and yet God feeds them. Of how much more value are you than the birds!" This, in turn, is part of a larger teaching by our Lord on the role of worry in our life in providing for our physical needs. "Can any of you by worrying add a single hour to your span of life? If then you are not able to do so small a thing as that, why do you worry about the rest? Consider the lilies, how they grow: they neither toil nor spin; yet I tell you, even Solomon in all his glory was not clothed like one of these. But if God so clothes the grass of the field, which is alive today and tomorrow is thrown into the oven, how much more will he clothe you—you of little faith! And do not keep striving for what you are to eat and what you are to drink, and do not keep worrying. For it is the nations of the world that strive after all these things, and your Father knows that you need them. Instead, strive for his kingdom, and these things will be given to you as well. Do not be afraid, little flock, for it is your Father's good pleasure to give you the kingdom. Sell your possessions, and give alms. Make purses for yourselves that do not wear out, an unfailing treasure in heaven, where no thief comes near and no moth destroys. For where your treasure is, there your heart will be also (Luke 12:22-34).

You may not have warmed up to ravens in these studies so far, but one thing they teach us is how we are to live. To be sure, the raven doesn't simply sit in its nest and wait for food to drop from the sky. In like manner, we are to be out and about, busy and productive—*ora et labora,* prayer and labor, as the monks used to say. But being busy is a very different than worrying. At the end of the day, promises Jesus, God will provide...no matter if you are a raven, or a prophet on the run.

DISCUSS/REFLECT

About what things in your life are you most likely to worry? Assuming you have experienced the truth Jesus proclaims—that worry is ultimately unable to produce meaningful results—what steps can you imagine taking to stop worrying?

What does it mean to "strive for God's Kingdom" instead of worrying? What specific steps can you take *today* to strive in that way?

READ

Talk about worry and stress! It seems that the whole point of Elijah's exile—first by the Kerith Brook, then in Zarephath—is to pass the time until God's appointed hour for *The Showdown*. This is one of the great stories of the Old Testament, and it starts when Elijah invites Ahab to assemble all of Israel at Mount Carmel, especially the 450 prophets of Baal (along with the four hundred prophets of Asherah, just to make it a real party).

READ

1 Kings 18:20-46 (the rest of the story found in 1 Kings 19:1-18 is worth reading later as well)

DISCUSS/REFLECT

What questions does this passage raise for you?

READ

It is a perfectly fair test: the prophets of Baal are given a bull, as is Elijah. Each is to prepare the sacrifice, build an altar, and then pray for fire to be sent down. At this point you need to know that Baal (meaning "owner" or "Lord") was a title particularly associated with Hadad, an Akkadian god of fertility, storm, and rain, often shown holding a thunderbolt (and so presumably in charge of "fire from the sky"), and often symbolized by a bull. The bull and lightening god is being offered the chance to burn a bull with lightening.

The prophets of Baal leap (or limp, depending on your translation), and cry out. Elijah prods them, suggesting that they cry louder in case their god is asleep or otherwise preoccupied (the phrase "wandered away" or "turned aside" could mean that he perhaps had to go relieve himself). The prophets seem to agree, and even cut themselves in a show of religious fervor and sacrifice, but to no avail. They raved on until the time of the offering, but there was no response from Baal.

Finally, it is Elijah's turn. He invites the people in to watch closely what he is doing, which is creating the most difficult conditions for the miracle to happen. But first, he repairs the altar of Yahweh, rebuilding it with twelve stones representative of Israel's heritage. Then he digs a trench around the altar, puts wood on it, then the bull. Then, in a season of drought, Elijah calls for four jars of water to be filled and poured out over the whole construction. This is done three times. We don't know how big the jars were, but the trench, which is full after the third soaking, was large enough to contain to two measures of seed, which is to say, about six gallons. Considering how dry the soil was to begin with, by the time the trench got full, the wood was so drenched that so there could be no claim of accidental spark.

That done, Elijah's simple prayer took less than thirty seconds. No repetitive cries, no leaping, and certainly no self-mutilation. A two-sentence prayer, and then fire fell, and consumed not only the bull and the wood, but even the stones, and most certainly the water! With this the people fell on their faces and said, "Yahweh indeed is God!"

Indeed: Yahweh can feed the ravens, and feed a prophet by way of the ravens. Yahweh can keep the meal in the jar and oil in the jug for as long as it takes (1 Kings 17:14). Yahweh can restore life to a widow's child (1 Kings 17:17-24). And Yahweh can bring holy fire down from heaven. If God can do all that, we don't need to worry. Yahweh is good, and His steadfast love endures forever. This is the oft-repeated affirmation of the Old Testament. Jesus reaffirms Yahweh's goodness and love in his preaching on the mount. "Consider the ravens: they neither sow nor reap, they have neither storehouse nor barn, and yet God feeds them. Of how much more value are you than the birds!" (Luke 12:24). Here is truth worth serious reflection: of how much more value are you than the birds!

DISCUSS/REFLECT

What insights and applications do you get from Elijah's face-off with the prophets of Baal?

In what ways have you seen the deliverance of God in your life through the years?

Do you agree with the Old Testament affirmation of God's goodness and steadfast love? Why or why not?

PRAYER

Conclude your time in prayer with and for one another.

They Shall Mount Up With Wings Like Eagles

DISCUSS/REFLECT

Have you ever seen an eagle in the wild? What was the occasion of the sighting, and how did it make you feel?

READ

Deuteronomy 32:10-12

DISCUSS/REFLECT

What questions does this passage raise for you?

READ

Eagles are mentioned frequently in scripture. In the prophetic literature the images are fearsome and threatening, but elsewhere the eagle, when used to represent Yahweh, is a bird of comfort and care. In the passage from Deuteronomy 32 we learn that God, like an eagle, "stirs the nest." This odd phrase may refer to the way in which eagles make the nest a less and less comfortable place as baby eaglets reach an age of departure. We also learn that, like an eagle, God hovers, wings spread, bearing us aloft. It turns out that baby eagles don't know how to fly, but must be taught.

In an oft-quoted passage, Frances Hamerstrom describes this process. She observed an eaglet for many days, noticing how the parents were present less and less, which meant the young bird was growing hungry. "Each time a parent came flying in toward the nest," she writes, 'he called for food eagerly; but over and over again, it came with empty feet, and the eaglet grew thinner. He pulled meat scraps from the old dried-up carcasses lying around the nest. He watched a sluggish carrion beetle, picked it up gingerly, and ate it. His first kill." She continues,

Days passed, and as he lost body fat he became quicker in his movements and paddled ever more lightly when the wind blew, scarcely touching the nest edge; from time to time he was airborne for a moment or two.

Parents often flew past and sometimes fed him. Beating his wings and teetering on the edge of the nest, he screamed for food whenever one flew by. And a parent often flew past just out of reach, carrying delectable meals: a half-grown jack rabbit or a plump rat raided from a dump. Although he was hungry almost all the time, he was becoming more playful as he lost his baby fat; sometimes, when no parent bird was in sight, he pounced ferociously on a scrap of prairie dog skin or on old bits of dried bone.

The male eaglet stayed by himself for the most part. He was no longer brooded at night. Hunger and the cold mountain nights were having their effect, not only on his body but on his disposition. A late frost hit the valley, and a night wind ruffled his feathers and chilled his body. When the sunlight reached the eyrie's (the brood in a nest of a bird of prey) edge, he sought its warmth; and soon, again, he was bounding in the wind, now light and firm-muscled.

A parent flew by, downwind, dangling a young marmot in its feet. The eaglet almost lost his balance in his eagerness for food. Then the parent swung by again, closer, upwind, and riding the updraft by the eyrie, as though daring him to fly. Lifted light by the wind, he was airborne, flying--or more gliding--for the first time in his life. He sailed across the valley to make a scrambling, almost tumbling landing on a bare knoll. As he turned to get his bearings the parent dropped the young marmot nearby. Half running, half flying he pounced on it, mantled, and ate his fill (prophetic. net/eagles.htm).

This is the image in Deuteronomy 32. God is caring for Israel, teaching her, and guiding her, just as God does also for us.

DISCUSS/REFLECT
Is it comforting or concerning that God's care for us includes "stirring up the nest." In what ways might God be trying to encourage you to fly at this moment?

READ
God's ability to care for us is largely found in God's ability to "see ahead" in our lives. The doctrine of God's providence is taken from the Latin word *provideo*, meaning to foresee and care.

Here's a fun fact: an eagle's eye weighs as much as a human eye. Human eyes occupy 5% of the head, but eagle eyes take up 50% of their heads. It has been noted that human eyes have 200,000 light sensitive cells per square millimeter of retina, but eagles have about one million such cells, all of which gives eagles a visual acuity virtually unsurpassed by any other creature. It is said that eagles have two sets of eyes, but it is more correct to say that they have two centers of focus, which allows them to see both forward and to the side at the same time. Eagles also have two sets of eyelids, one that closes for sleep, and another, called a nictitating membrane, that blinks to clean the eye, but which is translucent, so the eagle continues to see everything (baldeagleinfo.com/eagle2.html).

It is interesting that in a scene found in Revelation 4 depicting the heavenly throne room, there are four living creatures, one on each side of the throne of God. These four creatures—one like a lion, one like an ox, one like a human, and one like an eagle—each has six wings, are "full of eyes all around and inside..." (Revelation 4:8). This is odd anatomy to be sure, but the picture presented is clear: God sees everything, and in seeing all, knows our needs, and provides for us in due time.

DISCUSS/REFLECT
What evidence do you have from your past of God's providence and provision?

In looking forward in your life, what do you suppose God is seeing?

Can you imagine how God may be already providing for your future need, a need that God has foreseen?

READ

Isaiah 40:1-31

DISCUSS/REFLECT

What questions does this passage raise for you?

READ

The greater part of Isaiah 40, similar to the passage from Deuteronomy 32, takes up God's care and comfort of Israel. Having announced the bad news of Israel's captivity to Babylon, the prophet is now given a word of her release, and with it, word of God's tenderness toward His possession. The larger message of Isaiah 40 is of God's eternal power and purpose. God is up to something, and it has always been so. God is coming in strength like that of no other, and the series of questions that begin in verse 12 are proof of Yahweh's unique claim. "Even the nations are like a drop from a bucket...they are as nothing before him...to whom then will you liken God, or what likeness compare with him?" (vs 15, 17-18). The power of God is unmistakable, majestic, and marvelous, and is something that discerning people have faith have understood from the beginning: Yahweh has no equal (vs 25). "Have you not know? Have you not heard? The Lord is everlasting God, the Creator of the ends of the earth. He does not faint or grow weary; his understanding is unsearchable" (vs 28).

And because God is so great and so powerful, and at the same time so full of compassion, we get to the glorious culmination of this passage of comfort: "He gives power to the faint, and strengthens the powerless. Even youths will faint and be weary, and the young will fall exhausted; but those who wait for the Lord shall renew their strength, they shall mount up with wings like eagles, they shall run and not be weary, they shall walk and not faint" (vss 29-31).

This is indeed a glorious promise to those who are losing heart. The key, it seems, is in the waiting. As we all know, we are going to run out of steam, we are going to faint and lose power and be weary and fall exhausted. But those who *wait* for the Lord, those are the one who renew their strength, who mount up with wings like eagles. Good thing, because when we are fainting, powerless, weary and exhausted, waiting is about the only thing we can do!

Here's another fun fact: eagles are very patient. Eagles have been known to spot prey, watch it go into hiding, and then wait for hours for it to emerge. The problem for us is that we often don't value this time of waiting. We get impatient and feel like we have to produce. Waiting seems like a waste, a giving up. Let's agree that, while sometimes inactivity is worthless, waiting for the Lord is extremely worthwhile. It is an admission of our need; and a trusting of ourselves to the Only One who can help (have you not known, have you not heard?). To wait on the Lord is to do something very important: it is to put ourselves in a posture ready to receive from the Only One who can give.

It turns out that eagles themselves know something about this. Eagles are powerful fliers, but because they are so heavy, eagles can only sustain flight so long without the help of a thermal rise to carry them. Eagles first wait for the thermal and then wait for their prey, floating with ease and near effortlessness, thus renewing their strength for the next round of action (animals.mom.me /eagle-use-convection-currents-9206.html).

REFLECT/DISCUSS

Are you in a season of soaring or a season of sinking in your life right now?

What do you find to be the hardest part about waiting for the Lord?

What does "active waiting" look like? When and in whom have you seen it best demonstrated?

What would you imagine your next "thermal" to look like, or to feel like?

PRAYER

Conclude your time in prayer with and for one another.

His Eye Is On The Sparrow

DISCUSS/REFLECT

What do you know about sparrows?

READ

Matthew 6:25-34

DISCUSS/REFLECT

What questions does this passage raise for you?

READ

Jesus was a down to earth teacher...literally. He came to earth from his heavenly home, he met people on their own turf, and he taught us how to live in a plainspoken way. His teaching in the Sermon on the Mount is a great example of all of this, and that is where we find Jesus' teaching on worry.

As an aside, the birds that Jesus mentions in the Sermon on the Mount are...birds. Jesus uses the Greek word *peteina,* which is a generic term for a flying animal. (For the record, Luke 12:24 is a similar verse in which Jesus uses ravens, but enough with the ravens already!).

Jesus counsels us not to worry about food and drink, long life (health), or clothing. He offers simple, homespun examples, including the birds of the air, who don't worry about planting, but who get fed nonetheless. Some people might mis-interpret this teaching and think that they don't need to worry about having a job (which is how most of us pay for food and clothes). But that would be to miss not only Jesus' point, but also the larger teaching of Scripture. Read through the book of Proverbs and you will find plenty of advice about industry and effort, and plenty of condemnation of the foolish sluggard. Or this point, here's what the Apostle Paul says to the church at Thessalonica:

> For you yourselves know how you ought to imitate us; we were not idle when we were with you, and we did not eat anyone's bread without paying for it; but with toil and labor we worked night and day, so that we might not

burden any of you. This was not because we do not have that right, but in order to give you an example to imitate. For even when we were with you, we gave you this command: Anyone unwilling to work should not eat. For we hear that some of you are living in idleness, mere busybodies, not doing any work. Now such persons we command and exhort in the Lord Jesus Christ to do their work quietly and to earn their own living. Brothers and sisters, do not be weary in doing what is right (2 Thes 3:7-12).

Pretty hard to misinterpret that as freedom to just be a bird, or a lily, and lay back. Truth is, if you watch a bird for very long, you can see that it spends a good part of its time looking for food, which is the bird version of work!

So, what *is* Jesus saying? The key message is that, while we need to *work*, we don't need to *worry*. "Therefore do not worry," says Jesus, "your heavenly Father knows that you need all these things." And if we're not consumed with worry, focused on the negative, we are more free to focus on the positive, which is to seek first the kingdom of God and his righteousness. If we do that, Jesus says, things will have a way of working out.

So, what does it mean to seek first the kingdom of God? It means to live out of a particular mindset (we are forgiven and freed in Jesus Christ) in order to accomplish a particular mission (making disciples of all nations) in a particular way (according to two commandments Jesus gave—love God and love people).

DISCUSS/REFLECT

Jesus suggests many topics about which people might worry, including food and drink, long life (or health), and clothing. What are the things you tend to worry most about? What would Jesus say to you about those things?

What does "strive first for the kingdom of God and his righteousness" mean for you in your particular context?

READ

Matthew 10:29-31

DISCUSS/REFLECT

What questions does this passage raise for you?

READ

Do you know where the phrase "his eye is on the sparrow" appears in the Bible? Nowhere! Instead the beautiful phrase comes from the famous gospel song "His Eye Is on the Sparrow," written in 1905 by Civilla D. Martin. Civilla was on a trip to Elmira, New York, where she and her husband befriended a couple by the name of Mr. and Mrs. Doolittle. Apparently Mrs. Doolittle had been bedridden for almost twenty years, while her husband was himself confined to a wheelchair. Yet despite these difficulties, they were an inspiration of joy and comfort to all who knew them.

"One day while we were visiting with the Doolittles," Civilla would later write, "my husband commented on their bright hopefulness and asked them for the secret of it. Mrs. Doolittle's reply was simple: 'His eye is on the sparrow, and I know He watches me.'" The beauty of this simple summary of Matthew 10:29-30 gripped her heart, and a song was born (Vincent D. Homan, *A Foot in Two Worlds: A Pastor's Journey From Grief to Hope*, WestBow Press, 2013, p. 112).

For the record, sparrows are "perching" birds, a scientific designation that actually includes more than half of all birds, and refers to the arrangement of three toes pointing forward, one pointing back. The general description of sparrows is that they are small, brown and gray birds with short tails and stubby beaks. Pretty much ordinary in every way, and easy to overlook or take for granted. It is these common, humble birds who do not fall to the ground without God knowing, says Jesus. And so don't be afraid (and don't worry!), "you are of more value than many sparrows" (Matthew 10:31).

John Thomas Oakes is a composer, singer, and lover of Jesus. Some years ago he told a story in the Christian Reader about a chilly evening in Manhattan, when he and a friend were playing a Starbucks. During one of their songs Oakes noticed a lady sitting across the way, singing along. When they finished she approached and apologized for singing out loud. "Did it bother you?" she asked. "No," Oakes replied. "We love it when the audience joins in. Would you like to sing up front on the next selection?" And to his delight, she accepted. He offered her the chance to choose the song, and she asked if the duo knew any hymns. "Hymns? This woman didn't know who she was dealing with" says Oakes. "I cut my teeth on hymns. Before I was even born, I was going to church. I gave our guest singer a knowing look. 'Name one.'

"Oh, I don't know," she replied. "There are so many good ones. You pick one."

"Okay," said Oakes. "How about 'His Eye is on the Sparrow'?" His new friend didn't say anything, and glanced away for a moment. Then she looked Oakes in the eye and said, "Yeah. Let's do that one." She put down her purse, straightened her jacket and faced the center of the shop. After a two measure introduction she started to sing, "Why should I be discouraged? Why should the shadows come?" Oakes says, "The audience of coffee drinkers was transfixed."

The woman continued, "I sing because I'm happy; I sing because I'm free. For His eye is on the sparrow, and I know He watches me."

"When the last note was sung," says Oakes, "the applause crescendoed to a deafening roar. Embarrassed, the woman tried to shout over the din, 'Oh, y'all go back to your coffee! I didn't come in here to do a concert! I just came in here to get somethin' to drink, just like you!'

But the ovation continued. I embraced my new friend. "You, my dear, have made my whole year! That was beautiful!"

"It's funny that you picked that particular hymn," she said.

"Why is that?" asked Oakes.

She hesitated again, "that was my daughter's favorite song." She then grabbed Oakes hands. Things were quieting back down, and then the woman said, "She was 16. She died of a brain tumor last week."

Like most of us, Oakes didn't know quite what to say, and then asked, "Are you going to be okay?" The woman smiled through tear-filled eyes and squeezed his hands. "I'm gonna be okay. I've just got to keep trusting the Lord and singing His songs, and everything's gonna be just fine." And with that she picked up her bag, gave Oakes her card, and then was gone.

Oakes wonders if it might be just coincidence that he and his buddy happened to be singing in that particular coffee shop on that particular November night. He wonders if it was coincidence that this wonderful lady just happened to walk into that particular shop. He wonders if, of all the hymns to choose from, it wasn't just a coincidence that he happened to pick the favorite hymn of the woman whose daughter had just died the week before.

No, he doesn't think so. Instead Oakes affirms that God has his eye on all things (including the sparrows), and arranges "divine encounters" all the time, in this case turning an ordinary midtown Manhattan gig into a revival. "It was a great reminder," says Oakes, "that if we keep trusting Him and singing His songs, everything's gonna be okay (*Christian Reader,* date unknown).

DISCUSS/REFLECT
What comfort do you find in the knowledge that God's eye is on the sparrow?

PRAYER
Conclude your time in prayer with and for one another.

God the Mother Hen

DISCUSS/REFLECT

On a scale of one (*absolutely not!*) to ten (*completely fine!*), what is your personal level of comfort with considering feminine imagery when describing God?

READ

Luke 13:31-36

DISCUSS/REFLECT

What questions does this passage raise for you?

READ

Jesus says that he has often desired to gather the children of Jerusalem together "as a hen gathers her brood under her wings." There is no escaping the feminine imagery here, because Jesus uses the Greek word *ornis* which means "hen" and not the word *alektora* "rooster." (Compare Luke 22:61. For the record, all of the New Testament references to a male chicken are found in the passages referring to Peter's denial of Jesus. See next study)

There are several Old Testament passages speak of God showing this same kind of maternal care and concern:

Guard me as the apple of the eye; hide me in the shadow of your wings...

Psalm 17:8

How precious is your steadfast love, O God! All people may take refuge in the shadow of your wings.

Psalm 36:7

Be merciful to me, O God, be merciful to me, for in you my soul takes refuge; in the shadow of your wings I will take refuge, until the destroying storms pass by.

Psalm 57:1

Let me abide in your tent forever, find refuge under the shelter of your wings.

Psalm 61:4

...for you have been my help, and in the shadow of your wings I sing for joy.

Psalm 63:7

he will cover you with his pinions, and under his wings you will find refuge; his faithfulness is a shield and buckler.

Psalm 91:4

All of these would seem to add up to an acknowledgement that *God* is quite comfortable being thought of, at least now and then, in this feminine way. And while the Bible never uses the feminine gender for God, there are several other maternal images used in association with Yahweh throughout scripture (note that the first four quotes below are God speaking in the first person):

"Like a bear robbed of her cubs, I will attack them and rip them open," says the Lord.

Hosea 13:8

"For a long time I [God] have kept silent, I have been quiet and held myself back. But now, like a woman in childbirth, I cry out, I gasp and pant."

Isaiah 42:14

"As a mother comforts her child, so will I [God] comfort you; and you will be comforted over Jerusalem."

Isaiah 66:13

"Can a woman forget her nursing child, or show no compassion for the child of her womb? Even these may forget, yet I will not forget you."

Isaiah 49:15

My heart is not proud, LORD, my eyes are not haughty; I do not concern myself with great matters or things too wonderful for me. But I have calmed and quieted myself, I am like a weaned child with its mother; like a weaned child I am content. Israel, put your hope in the LORD both now and forevermore.

Psalm 131

DISCUSS/REFLECT

Of the verses above, either having to do with protection under the wings of God, or those more generally suggesting a maternal side of God, which do you find most comforting? Which do you find most disturbing or difficult?

Do you agree or disagree that God is comfortable being thought of, at least occasionally, in this feminine way? Why or why not?

READ

Luke 15:8-10

DISCUSS/REFLECT

What questions does this passage raise for you?

READ

Other than Jesus suggesting he would like to gather the children of Jerusalem under his wings like a mother hen, perhaps nothing else in the New Testament gets at this issue of the feminine side of God like the story of the woman householder in Luke 15. This short description of God's relentless love for us is usually overshadowed by the two others it sits between. In the first, God is described as a shepherd who leaves his 99 sheep in order to find the one that is lost. In the third, God is described as father to a prodigal son, who tirelessly goes to the edge of town every day to watch for his son's return.

But in the middle story, Jesus talks about a woman who loses one of her ten silver coins. And if we clearly understand the first and third parables to be about the relentless and searching love of God, then we must also understand the middle parable in the same way. And in the parable, God the searching *woman* first prepares to search by lighting a lamp, then sweeps the house (ancient middle eastern homes usually had dirt floors, over which was spread a layer of straw to keep the dust down). Once she has done all that, the woman searches *diligently*. As urgent as the shepherd seeking a lost sheep, as tireless as a father waiting for a prodigal son, this woman searches diligently until the lost coin is found.

Again, to be clear, nowhere in scripture is a female pronoun used in reference to God, as doing so would have been out of touch with the patriarchal context of the Bible. But Jesus was constantly doing and saying subversive things that upset the status quo and pointed to the truth. This is no different. Jesus isn't inventing a new category: as we've seen, there are many Old Testament images of God's maternal way with us. But Jesus is clearly hoping to invite his hearers to expand their thinking about who God is. Images of God the Father, Christ the Son, will always dominate our Christian faith, and rightly so, but by seeing the maternal images throughout the Bible we help deepen our understanding of God's way with us.

DISCUSS/REFLECT

Has your level of comfort with considering feminine imagery when describing God changed? Where are you now on the 1-10 scale?

How is your faith enlarged, or your understanding of God's character made deeper, by these images?

PRAYER

Conclude your time in prayer with and for one another.

For Whom the Cock Crows

DISCUSS/REFLECT

What is your best guess as to why the chicken crossed the road?

READ

John 13:37-38

DISCUSS/REFLECT

What questions does this passage raise for you?

READ

Believe it or not, there is a considerable amount of scholarship about the origin of the domesticated chicken, and believe it or not, there is not complete agreement on the matter! It seems certain that all chickens are descended from the Red Junglefowl, a bird indigenous to a swath of land from northern Pakistan, through India and Myanmar, and reaching into China, Thailand, and Vietnam. But it is uncertain exactly when and where chickens were first raised domestically, and it is possible this happened in diverse places.

Whenever and wherever it happened, it seems chickens may have arrived in the Middle East around 1000 B.C.E, but were at first considered exotic, and used primarily in pagan worship and cockfights. Since chickens are not named in the lists of birds forbidden for food in Leviticus 11:13-19 and Deuteronomy 14:11-18, there was no barrier to their consumption as food. Indeed, the earliest evidence of chickens in Israel comes by way of a rooster image cut into the handle of a cooking pot discovered at Gibeon and dating to the seventh century B.C.E. (jerusalemperspective.com). A collection of chicken bones found in the ancient city of Lachish and dating to about 300 B.C.E., suggests that poultry was by then being bred for commercial purposes in the region (jpost.com).

According to scholar Joshua Tilton, roosters played an important role in the ancient world as time-keepers. He notes that Pliny the Elder called chickens "skilled astronomers," as it was these birds who helped wake workers before dawn and get the world moving once more. This time keeping function is even encoded into the timing of various Temple activities, such as the removal of the ashes from the altar, required to take place "at cockcrow" (see also Mark 13:35) (jerusalemperspective.com).

As it happens, however, it wasn't until 2013 that scientists began to understand what it is about chickens that made them so skilled at time keeping. The current working theory is that chickens aren't responding to day break, but an internal circadian clock that is timed to 23.8 hours (cell.com/current-biology).

All of which brings us to Peter's denial, and perhaps the most famous chicken in the Bible. Jesus says that Peter will deny Him three times before the cock crows, which is to say, three times before day break. It turns out Peter had a long night, in fact, it seems that he was up all night.

READ

John 18:15-18, 25-27

DISCUSS/REFLECT

What questions does this passage raise for you?

READ

Staying up all night, being under high stress, these are the conditions for unfortunate choices. In his commentary on this passage, William Barclay notes that the difference between Judas and Peter is that the betrayal of Judas was quite deliberate. Judas had time to plan, and he carried out his plan while looking Jesus straight in the eye. Peter, on the other hand, denied Jesus in a moment of weakness, tiredness, and duress. There is a difference, suggests Barclay, between sin that is deliberately calculated, and sin which involuntarily conquers us in a moment of weakness. There is a difference, he says, between the sin that knows what it is doing, and the sin that comes when we are so weak or inflamed that we scarcely know what we are doing at all.

No doubt, sin is sin, and all sin needs the blood of the cross. But reading the Old Testament laws on atonement make it clear that not all sin is the same before God. We read in about this in Numbers 15:

"But if you unintentionally fail to observe all these commandments that the Lord has spoken to Moses— everything that the Lord has commanded you by Moses, from the day the Lord gave commandment and thereafter, throughout your generations—then if it was done unintentionally without the knowledge of the congregation, the whole congregation shall offer one young bull for a burnt offering, a pleasing odor to the Lord, together with its grain offering and its drink offering, according to the ordinance, and one male goat for a sin offering…. But whoever acts high-handedly, whether a native or an alien, affronts the Lord, and shall be cut off from among the people. Because of having despised the word of the Lord and broken his commandment, such a person shall be utterly cut off and bear the guilt (vs 22-24, 30-31).

DISCUSS/REFLECT

What is the practical result of making a distinction between intentional and unintentional sin? To put it another way, while we all need the forgiveness that only Christ can offer, does it matter how we view ourselves if we are able to distinguish between intentional and accidental sin?

READ

John 21:1-14

DISCUSS/REFLECT

What questions does this passage raise for you?

READ

Jesus arranges to meet Peter "just after daybreak." In other words, there might not have been any roosters crowing, but it was early in the morning. Furthermore, as noted in *Famous Fish of the Bible,* there is an interesting detail about the fire Jesus has started on the beach. John tells us that it is a "charcoal fire" (in Greek, *anthrakia),* and he is being very intentional. John assumes we are hearing this story told from beginning to end, and that we will remember the part when Peter was standing in the courtyard of the high priest. John also assumes we will remember that it was cold that night, and so Peter and everyone else was standing around a *charcoal* fire." In other words, the only two places in John's story where we hear about *charcoal* fires (and in fact, the only two times the word is used at all in the New Testament), is first, at the time of Peter's denial, and second, at the time of his restoration.

After breakfast, after staring at that charcoal fire for what must have seemed like a lifetime, Jesus gives Peter three chances to affirm his love, three chances to receive forgiveness—one for each of Peter's three denials. It's a tender, touching scene, in which Peter is led, one denial at a time, through a process of healing, and is restored and set free for service. What could be have been a confrontation becomes a commission, what could have been just a clam bake becomes communion (*Famous Fish of the Bible*, Brant Baker).

DISCUSS/REFLECT

Do you think there is a connection between forgiveness and commission in the lives of all Christians? Can you think of other examples of someone being forgiven by Jesus and then commissioned in some particular way (either in the Bible or throughout the history of Christianity)?

For your own reflection: can you make that same connection in your own life? What has Christ forgiven, and what is He now calling you to do?

PRAYER

Conclude your time in prayer with and for one another.

Other books and studies by Brant Baker

Famous Fish of the Bible

Famous Cows of the Bible

Famous Donkeys of the Bible

Wine in the Bible

The Rest of the Story, Vols 1-3

50 Skills You Need for a Decent Chance of Success

Hands-On Christianity: Eight Studies for Small Groups

The Gamer Bible Study: Six Studies for Teens

The Abingdon Children's Sermon Library (3 vols) (Editor)

Let the Children Play

Teaching People to Pray

The Jesus Story (with Ben Johnson)

Welcoming The Children

Let the Children Come

Find them all on Amazon!

Printed in the USA
CPSIA information can be obtained
at www.ICGtesting.com
LVHW092025150424
777462LV00005B/725